Music Theory Past Papers 2015
Model Answers

ABRSM Grade 4

Welcome to ABRSM's *Music Theory Past Papers 2015 Model Answers*, Grade 4. These answers are a useful resource for students and teachers preparing for ABRSM theory exams and should be used alongside the relevant published theory past papers.

All the answers in this booklet would receive full marks but not all possible answers have been included for practicable reasons. In these cases other reasonable alternatives may also be awarded full marks. For composition-style questions (where candidates must complete a rhythm, compose a melody based on a given opening or set text to music) only one example of the many possible answers is given.

For more information on how theory papers are marked and some general advice on taking theory exams, please refer to the Music Theory Grade 4 web page: www.abrsm.org/theory4.

Using these answers

- Answers are given in the same order and, where possible, in the same layout as in the exam papers, making it easy to match answer to question.

- Where it is necessary to show the answer on a stave, the original stave is printed in grey with the answer shown in black, for example:

- Alternative answers are separated by an oblique stroke (/) or by *or*, for example:

  getting slower / gradually getting slower

- The old-style crotchet rest ⌐ is accepted as a valid alternative to the modern symbol ⌡ .

- Answers that require the candidate to write out a scale or chord have been shown at one octave only. Reasonable alternatives at different octaves can also receive full marks.

- Sometimes the clef, key and time signature of the relevant bar(s) are included for added clarity, for example:

© 2016 by The Associated Board of the Royal Schools of Music
Published by ABRSM (Publishing) Ltd, a wholly owned subsidiary of ABRSM
Cover by Kate Benjamin & Andy Potts
Printed in England by Halstan & Co. Ltd, Amersham, Bucks

Theory Paper   Grade 4   2015   A
Model Answers

1 (a) fast / quick / cheerful / lively   (2)
          more   (2)

   (b) fourteen   (2)

   (c) X   minor 3rd   (2)
        Y   perfect 4th   (2)

   (d)    (2)

   (e) 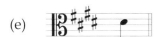   (3)

2 *There are many ways of completing this question. Either of the specimen completions below would receive full marks.* (10)

EITHER

   (a)

        In   this   wa - ter clear   as   air   Lurks   a   lob-ster   in   its   lair.

Text reproduced by permission of the Literary Trustees of Walter de la Mare
and The Society of Authors as their representative.

OR

   (b)

3 (a) (i) rather slow / slow but not as slow as Largo   (2)
                semi-staccato / slightly detached / slightly separated   (2)
                getting softer / dying away   (2)

        (ii)    (2)

        (iii) false   (2)

3

(b) (i) X supertonic (2)
Y submediant (2)
(ii) F minor (2)

(iii) 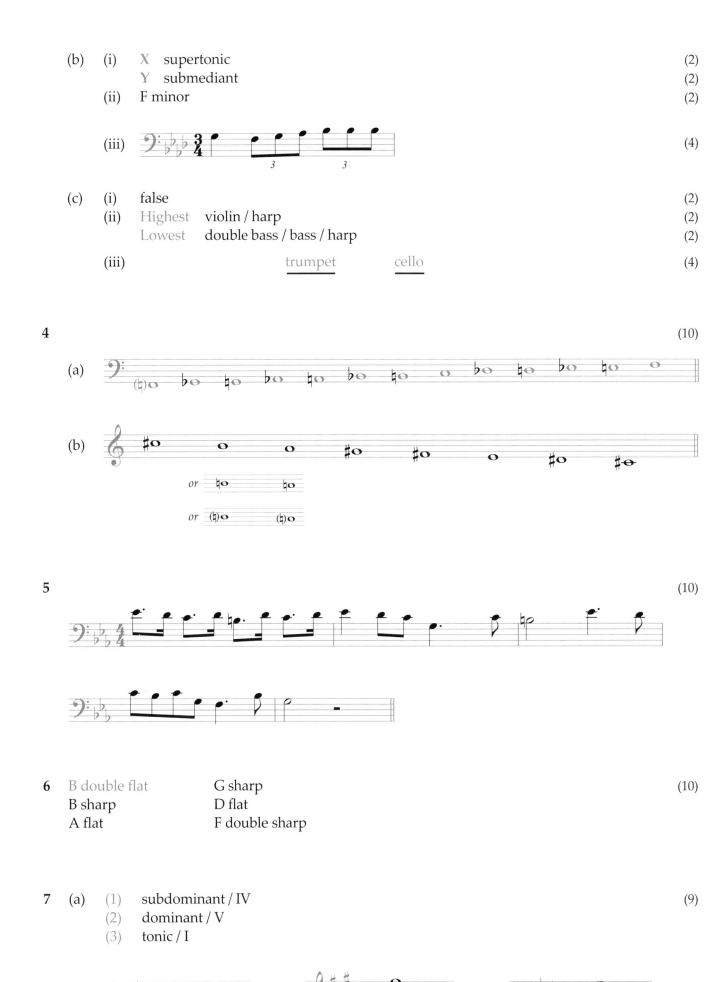 (4)

(c) (i) false (2)
(ii) Highest violin / harp (2)
Lowest double bass / bass / harp (2)

(iii) trumpet cello (4)

4 (10)

(a)

(b)

or

or

5 (10)

6 B double flat G sharp (10)
B sharp D flat
A flat F double sharp

7 (a) (1) subdominant / IV (9)
(2) dominant / V
(3) tonic / I

(b) (6)

Theory Paper   Grade 4   2015   B
Model Answers

1   (a)   tenderly / affectionately   (2)

      (b)   simple   (1)
            duple   (1)

      (c)   E   (2)

      (d)   G major   (2)

      (e)   twelve   (2)

      (f)   mordent / upper mordent   (2)

      (g)    (3)

2   *There are many ways of completing this question. Either of the specimen completions below would receive full marks.*   (10)

EITHER

      (a)

OR

      (b)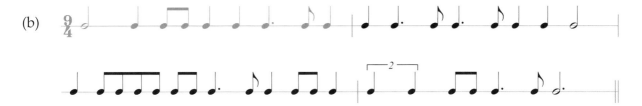

3   (a)   (i)   *lent*   (2)

           (ii)   *There are two possible answers to this question. Either of the answers shown would receive full marks.*   (2)

           (iii)   harmonic   (2)

(iv)  (2)

(v) (2)

(b) (i)  (2)

(ii)  (4)

(iii) *There are two possible answers to this question. Either of the answers shown would receive full marks.* (2)

(iv) 8; 9 (2)

(c) (i) String   violin / harp (2)
        Woodwind   flute / oboe / clarinet (2)
(ii) tuba / bass tuba (2)
(iii) false (2)
     true (2)

4 (10)

(a)

(b)

5 (10)

6 1 perfect 4th (10)
  2 augmented 2nd
  3 major 6th
  4 diminished 5th
  5 minor 7th

7 (a) (1) tonic / I (9)
    (2) subdominant / IV
    (3) dominant / V

  (b) B major   A minor   B♭ major (6)
    tonic / I   dominant / V   subdominant / IV

Theory Paper   Grade 4   2015   C
Model Answers

1 (a) slow / stately (2)
    sad (2)
    with mutes / muted (2)

  (b) *The answer is shown by square brackets on the extract reproduced above.* (2)

  (c) *There are two possible answers to this question. Either of the circles shown on the extract reproduced above* (2)
    would receive full marks.

  (d) dominant (2)

  (e) (3)

2 *There are many ways of completing this question. Either of the specimen completions below would receive full marks.* (10)

EITHER

  (a) An   ap - ple pie,   when   it looks nice,   Would make one long   to have a   slice.

OR

  (b)

3 (a) (i) slight pressure / slight accent / slight emphasis / slightly separated / hold the note for its full value (2)

   (ii) *vivo* *animato* (4)

   (iii) 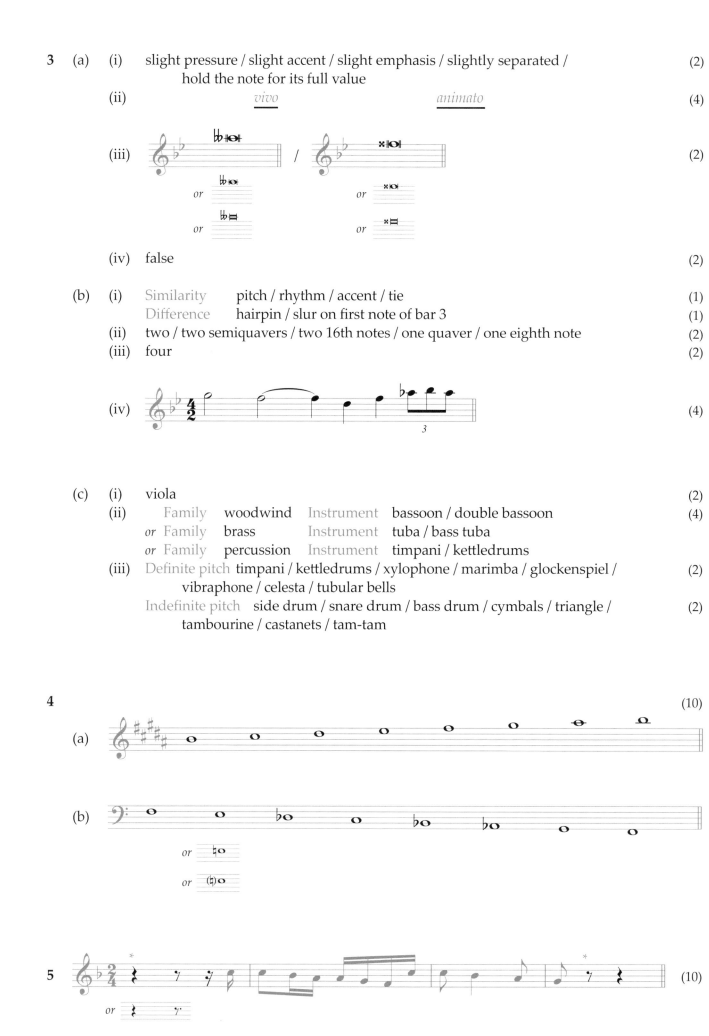 / (2)

   (iv) false (2)

(b) (i) Similarity pitch / rhythm / accent / tie (1)
        Difference hairpin / slur on first note of bar 3 (1)
   (ii) two / two semiquavers / two 16th notes / one quaver / one eighth note (2)
   (iii) four (2)

   (iv) (4)

(c) (i) viola (2)
   (ii) Family woodwind Instrument bassoon / double bassoon (4)
        or Family brass Instrument tuba / bass tuba
        or Family percussion Instrument timpani / kettledrums
   (iii) Definite pitch timpani / kettledrums / xylophone / marimba / glockenspiel / vibraphone / celesta / tubular bells (2)
        Indefinite pitch side drum / snare drum / bass drum / cymbals / triangle / tambourine / castanets / tam-tam (2)

4 (10)

(a)

(b)
        or
        or

5 (10)
   or

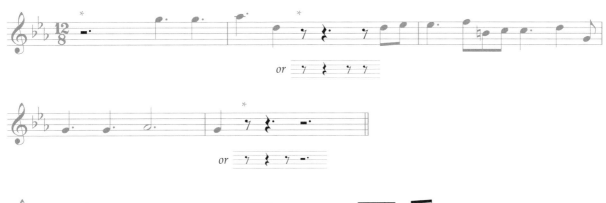

6  (10)

7 (a) (1) tonic / I   (9)
       (2) dominant / V
       (3) subdominant / IV

   (b) 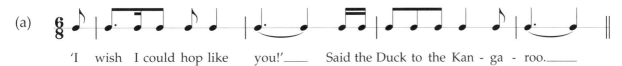 (6)

Theory Paper   Grade 4   2015   S
Model Answers

1 (a) sweet / gentle   (2)
        very sustained / much sustained   (4)

   (b)   (2)

   (c)  (4)

   (d) A   (1)

   (e) twenty   (2)

2 *There are many ways of completing this question. Either of the specimen completions below would receive full marks.* (10)

EITHER

   (a) 'I wish I could hop like   you!'____ Said the Duck to the Kan - ga - roo.____

OR

(b)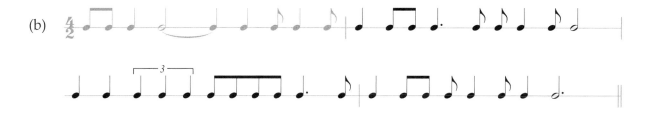

3 (a) (i) in a singing style (2)

forced / forcing / accented (2)

(ii)  *lent* (2)

(iii) (4)

(b)

(i) *There are three possible answers to this question. Any of the brackets shown above would receive full marks.* (2)

(ii) F (2)

(iii) appoggiatura / leaning note (2)

(iv) 7 (2)

(v) *There are three possible answers to this question. Any of the circles shown above would receive full marks.* (2)

(c) (i) String violin / harp (2)

Woodwind flute / oboe / clarinet (2)

(ii) tuba / bass tuba (2)

(iii) *trumpet* *viola* (4)

4   (10)

(a)

(b)

5   (10)

(a)

(b)

6   (10)

(a)

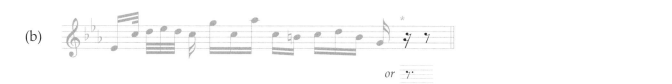

(b)

7 (a) (1) tonic / I   (9)
         (2) dominant / V
         (3) subdominant / IV

(b)   (6)

Music Theory Past Papers 2015 Model Answers

Model answers for four past papers from ABRSM's 2015 Theory exams for Grade 4

Key features:

- a list of correct answers where appropriate
- a selection of likely options where the answer can be expressed in a variety of ways
- a single exemplar where a composition-style answer is required

Support material for ABRSM Theory exams

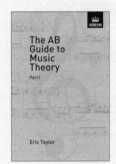

ABRSM
24 Portland Place
London W1B 1LU
United Kingdom

www.abrsm.org

ABRSM is the exam board of the Royal Schools of Music. We are committed to actively supporting high-quality music-making, learning and development throughout the world, and to producing the best possible resources for music teachers and students.

I S B N 978-1-84849-750-4